D1473490

A Celebration of the Civil Rights Movement ™

THE NAACP: A CELEBRATION

Diane Bailey

ROSEN
PUBLISHING®

New York

Published in 2015 by The Rosen Publishing Group, Inc.
29 East 21st Street, New York, NY 10010

Library of Congress Cataloging-in-Publication Data

Bailey, Diane, 1966–
The NAACP: a celebration/Diane Bailey.
    pages cm. – (A celebration of the civil rights movement)
Includes bibliographical references and index.
ISBN 978-1-4777-7747-3 (library bound)
1. National Association for the Advancement of Colored People—History. 2. African Americans—History—19th century. 3. African Americans–History—20th century. 4. African Americans—Civil rights—History—19h century. 5. African Americans—Civil rights—History—20th century. 6. Civil rights movements—United States—History—19th century. 7. Civil rights movements—United States—History—20th century. I. Title.
E185.61.B137 2015
973'.0496073—dc23

                                    2013046771

Manufactured in the United States of America

CONTENTS

which shall be determined by adding to the whole Number
three fifths of all other Persons. The actual Enumeration
within every subsequent Term of ten Years, in such Manner as
Thousand, but each State shall have at Least one
to chuse three, Massachusetts eight, Rhode Island and
Delaware one, Maryland six, Virginia ten, North Carolina
When vacancies happen in the Representation from any
The House of Representatives shall chuse their Speaker and

NAACP
NATIONAL ASSOCIATION FOR THE ADVANCEMENT OF COLORED PEOPLE
NAACP
FOUNDED
1909
www.naacp.org

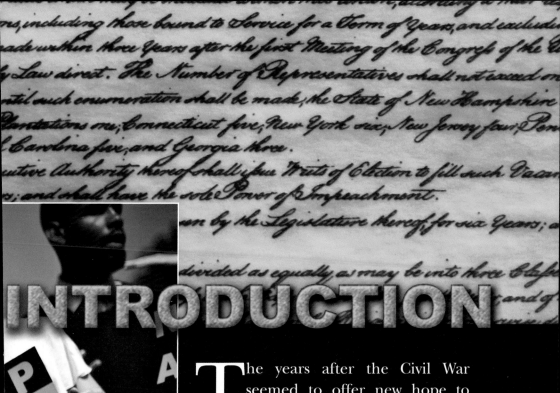

INTRODUCTION

The years after the Civil War seemed to offer new hope to America's black citizens. During the war, President Abraham Lincoln had freed the slaves in the Southern states with his Emancipation Proclamation (1863). Two years later, the Constitution was amended to abolish slavery. Later constitutional amendments guaranteed blacks the right to vote and the right to fair treatment under the law. It all looked good on paper—but Jim Crow had other ideas.

Jim Crow was not a real person. Rather, he was a character from a minstrel show. The name was adopted

Members of the National Association for the Advancement of Colored People (NAACP) demonstrate in front of the U.S. Supreme Court on June 25, 2013. On this day, the Court struck down part of the Voting Rights Act designed to protect the rights of African Americans.

because it presented a negative image of blacks. In the Southern states, "Jim Crow laws" robbed blacks of many rights. These laws segregated blacks from whites in public places, and the two races were often forbidden to interact. Where whites were allowed to own property, blacks were not. Where whites were allowed to be out after dark, blacks were not. Blacks were sometimes the victims of lynch mobs. Crowds of white people would accuse a black person of some crime, often with no evidence, and then seek "justice" through torture and murder. In fact, forty years after the Civil War, blacks were losing ground in terms of their rights as citizens.

A major blow came in 1896 with a decision by the U.S. Supreme Court in the case of *Plessy v. Ferguson*. In this case, the Court ruled that individual states could pass laws that required blacks and whites to use separate facilities, as long as those facilities were equal to one another. The case was about train seating, but the decision was applied to everything from drinking fountains to restrooms to entire schools. The phrase "separate but equal" from the ruling became the new standard. However, in practice, black facilities were not even close to equal to white ones.

African Americans knew something had to change, but it was clear that America's white-dominated society wasn't going to do it voluntarily. Blacks would have to fight for true equality. It was in this climate that the National Association for the Advancement of Colored People (NAACP) began. At first, the association had few members and little money. But the founders had plenty of passion and determination. They had a vision for a country that would not be defined and divided by racist practices.

Today, more than one hundred years later, the NAACP has grown from a handful of activists to a membership of some 425,000. During those years, it won landmark legal cases that finally gave blacks the equal rights to which they were entitled, from education to employment to housing. There were plenty of roadblocks along the way, as the NAACP tackled a society that was almost entirely controlled by whites. Hostilities sometimes escalated into violence and even murder. In many cases, it would have been easier for African Americans to step back and stay silent. Change would be difficult, but with the NAACP's help, it was not impossible. Of course, no law or court decision can eradicate racist attitudes, but over the past century, the NAACP consistently has acted intelligently, patiently, and tirelessly. It helped prove to the world that African Americans deserved not only rights, but also respect.

Chapter 1

ANSWERING THE CALL

In 1906, a unit of black soldiers stationed in Brownsville, Texas, ran up against white hostility in the segregated town. A fight broke out, and the soldiers were banned from entering the city limits. Several days later, a shooting occurred in which one white man was killed and another injured. Even though some witnesses said the black soldiers were nowhere near the area at the time, they were blamed for the incident and discharged from the army.

INCREASING TENSIONS

On the heels of this event came a race riot in Atlanta, Georgia, which had a large black population. Blacks and whites were competing with each other for jobs, and as blacks gained more power and rights, it made whites uncomfortable. Eventually, the hostility exploded into a riot in which dozens of African Americans were killed or wounded. Two years later, in 1908, another race riot erupted in Springfield, Illinois. There, a mob of white people tried to attack two black prisoners accused of crimes against whites. When the mob discovered

21 WEST 38TH STREET

New York, Feb. 6, 1909.

My dear Mr. Baker,

The enclosed statement to the public and call for a National Conference (which it is suggested should be held in May or June) speaks for itself.

I have been instructed by those who have already signed this document to send it to some seventy persons. If the large majority of these persons are heard from, as we expect, by Lincoln's birthday, the statement will be issued to the public at that very auspicious moment.

The statement has just been brought into its present form, but already it has received a number of signatures, including those of Miss Jane Addams, Rev. Dr. Parkhurst, Oswald Garrison Villard, Professor Charles D. Zueblin, Rev. John Haynes Holmes, Rabbi Stephen S. Wise, Bishop Walters and W. E. B. DuBois, while no person to whom it has been submitted has hesitated to sign it.

We need your support and confidently count upon a favorable reply, obviously at your very earliest convenience.

Very respectfully yours,

Wm English Walling
Sec.

In 1909, several prominent community leaders—both black and white—made an appeal to hold a conference focusing on the rights of African American citizens.

the prisoners had already been moved to a safe location, they turned their rage upon the city's black population in general. Thousands of black residents hid or ran to escape.

When would the next riot be? How many would die then? It wasn't just blacks who were worried. Many forward-thinking white citizens were also concerned about the fate of blacks in a society that was becoming more polarized. The Springfield riot had occurred in the North, where racism was not even as intense as it was in the South. It was also symbolic that Springfield was the hometown of President Lincoln—a man who had done much to help the black race. If violence could happen there, in a Northern city, where would it end?

In 1909, several people met in New York City. Some were black, some were white, but all of them were concerned about the future of African Americans. Among them were Mary White Ovington, a white liberal activist, and William English Walling, a white liberal journalist who, notably, came from the South. Also joining the cause were social worker Henry Moskowitz; W. E. B. Du Bois, an influential black leader; and Ida B. Wells, a black journalist who worked to prevent lynching. They chose February 12, 1909, the one hundredth anniversary of Lincoln's birthday, to issue "The Call," a document beseeching concerned citizens to form a group to fight racial injustice. The group was initially called the National Negro Committee. At its first annual conference in the spring of 1909, several leaders gathered to try to disprove the commonly believed notion that African Americans were inferior to whites. Indeed, that was the root of the issue: blacks had to be seen as equals. The next year, the group changed its name to the National Association for the Advancement of Colored People (NAACP).

THE NIAGARA MOVEMENT

In 1905, W. E. B. Du Bois invited several dozen well-known African Americans to a meeting held in Niagara Falls, Canada. His purpose was to bring together black leaders to examine the problem of racism in America and to band together to fight it. The so-called Niagara Movement is often considered the forerunner of the NAACP. While the initial attendees were all black, a year later several white people joined the cause. The Niagara Movement never fully got off the ground, partly due to lack of money and a unified philosophy. However, several members of the Niagara Movement later helped form the NAACP.

BREAKING AWAY FROM BOOKER

At the time, few blacks had a respected presence in a white-dominated society, but one who did was Booker T. Washington. For that reason, it was notable that he didn't attend the NAACP's first meetings. Washington was born into slavery in 1856. After the Civil War, he became a leading advocate of black advancement. However, he believed that African Americans should try to improve their opportunities for education and jobs, rather than fight for desegregation and racial equality. In 1895, Washington delivered a speech at the Atlanta Exposition that became known as the "Atlanta Compromise." He encouraged blacks to pursue basic vocational education

W. E. B. Du Bois was a prominent black scholar and leader in the early 1900s. One of the founders of the NAACP, he served on its board of directors and edited *The Crisis*, its monthly magazine.

and get jobs, not fight the overall pattern of social segregation. He believed that as more blacks contributed as productive members of society, civil and political equality would follow. However, this approach did not sit well with other African American leaders, especially W. E. B. Du Bois.

In 1903, Du Bois published a book of essays titled *The Souls of Black Folk*, in which he wrote what it was really like to be black in a racist society. He also promoted the idea of the "Talented Tenth," arguing that fully 10 percent of black Americans could—and should—take positions of responsibility and leadership.

Du Bois wanted the NAACP to take a much firmer stance than Washington did. He believed the organization should not make concessions in an effort not to threaten white America. Instead, it should directly fight the problems of segregation and racism. Du Bois's attitude, though somewhat radical for its time, would provide the moral basis of the NAACP.

Some early supporters were worried about excluding Washington. They felt he was needed to attract influential white people who could help the new organization. In its early years, the NAACP still depended heavily on the efforts of white people. In U.S. society in that period, blacks simply did not command enough respect and power to make changes without the support of whites. However, even without Washington, who opposed the NAACP's aggressive philosophy, the association took root.

The NAACP operated with a grassroots approach. It raised money by charging its members $1 annually in dues, and it used a lot of volunteers. The organization depended heavily on publicizing injustices in order to raise awareness and gain support. It began publishing a magazine, *The Crisis*, which was

A recruiter finds a new member for the NAACP in 1945. By keeping its annual dues to an affordable $1 until 1949, the NAACP was able to build its membership significantly.

edited by Du Bois. *The Crisis*, which focused on issues important to blacks, became an important tool that the NAACP used to reach its members. It is still being published more than one hundred years later.

FIRST STEPS

The NAACP immediately began to champion the rights of blacks, especially their legal rights. This strategy would come to define the association's approach for the next half century. The organization was new. It didn't have that many members, and it didn't have much money. Still, in 1910, it took on its first legal challenge with the case of Pink Franklin, a black sharecropper. Franklin's employer had accused him of accepting money for work and then moving away. When police went to Franklin's home in the middle of the night to arrest him, Franklin killed an officer. He defended himself by saying the officer had not identified himself, and he thought he was a burglar. Nonetheless, Franklin was sentenced to death. The NAACP intervened. It managed to have Franklin's sentence reduced to life in prison, and he eventually earned his freedom in 1919.

The NAACP also began to attack other practices that discriminated against blacks. In 1915, the organization successfully fought an Oklahoma voting law, participating in the Supreme Court case that struck it down. The state had a literacy test that voters had to pass. However, a "grandfather clause" created an exception. Men whose grandfathers had been eligible to vote in 1866 were also allowed to vote, even if they could not pass the literacy test. However, most blacks' grandfathers would not have been eligible to vote in 1866. That meant the law favored whites over blacks.

A poster advertising D. W. Griffith's 1915 movie *Birth of a Nation* shows a member of the Ku Klux Klan. The NAACP criticized the silent film for its racist messages, but it was still a box-office hit.

While the NAACP was making some legal inroads, changing public opinion would be a much more difficult task. In 1915, filmmaker D. W. Griffith released *Birth of a Nation*. In the film, blacks were portrayed as stupid, while the anti-black organization the Ku Klux Klan was celebrated. The NAACP protested at screenings of the movie, but it was well-received by the public.

IN THE TRENCHES

World War I (1914–1918) had a profound effect on race relations in the United States. During the war, the NAACP worked hard to improve soldiers' rights and opportunities. When the United States entered the war in 1917, the army allowed blacks to enlist, but they were forced to live in separate accommodations and could not train with the white soldiers. The navy allowed blacks only as kitchen help. The other branches of the military would not admit them at all.

BEING HEARD

Civil rights activist James Weldon Johnson was an early leader within the NAACP. He was also an accomplished writer. In 1900, as part of a celebration for Lincoln's birthday, he wrote a poem called "Lift Ev'ry Voice and Sing." Johnson's brother set the poem to music, and in 1919, the NAACP adopted it, calling it the Negro National Anthem. In the 1990s, it was entered into the Congressional Record as the Black National Anthem.

The NAACP lobbied to get more blacks admitted into the armed forces. To do so, it made a major concession, submitting to the reality that blacks would be trained in separate facilities. The association was divided on whether to give in to segregation, but in the end it decided that it was a necessary step to get blacks the right to serve in the military at all.

Although thousands of African Americans did end up serving in World War I, breaking the color barrier was not a perfect

A group of African American soldiers returns to the United States from Europe in 1918 after fighting in World War I. They are wearing medals awarded for bravery in battle.

success by any means. In many cases, African Americans were only allowed to do lower-level tasks, even when they had the knowledge and training to do more complex or specialized jobs. There were hundreds of complaints of abuse and racism. Black soldiers who went into combat were sometimes accused of cowardice and crimes in the line of duty.

Conditions did not improve upon the return of the soldiers at the end of the war. Black troops were proud of their accomplishments in Europe, and they had been fighting for the cause of democracy. They expected democracy in America as well. Instead, they returned to the same racism that they had left. Du Bois wrote in an editorial in *The Crisis* that the war would be tougher at home than abroad, and that soldiers should expect "to fight a sterner, longer, more unbending battle" on their home soil. Indeed, these words would describe the next several decades in the fight for civil rights.

Chapter 2

A CRUSADE AGAINST VIOLENCE

In 1899, a young black man named Sam Hose killed his boss, a white man. Though the act was in self-defense, Hose knew he would receive little protection from the white community in rural Georgia. He tried to leave town, but he was not fast enough. A mob of whites caught him before he could get away. The lynching that followed was a frightening example of mob behavior. Hose was beaten, mutilated, and finally burned alive. But perhaps far worse than his individual story was that he was only one of many black people who suffered a similar fate.

By the 1910s and 1920s, the NAACP was focused on the growing problem of lynching. Violence against blacks, especially in the South, was widespread. Few efforts were being made to stop it, but the NAACP was determined to try.

THIRTY YEARS TOO MANY

Another horrific lynching occurred in Waco, Texas, in 1916. Jesse Washington, a black teenager, confessed to raping and murdering his employer's wife. (Later investigations showed

Far too often, the NAACP hung a sobering banner from the window of its New York City headquarters to raise awareness of the problem of lynching.

he could have been innocent but was pressured to confess.) A lightning-fast trial resulted. A jury took only four minutes to convict him and hand down a death sentence. But before authorities could remove him from the courtroom, a mob pushed them aside and dragged Washington outside. They proceeded to beat him, dismember his body, and burn him to death. The event attracted national attention, in part because the whole thing had been photographed as it was occurring. Newspapers across the country condemned the terrible act.

After this event, the NAACP investigated the incident and began an anti-lynching campaign in earnest. One practice it started was to hang a banner from the window of its New York office whenever it learned of a new incident. Upon a black background, stark white letters proclaimed: "A Man Was Lynched Yesterday."

In 1918, the NAACP published a book, *Thirty Years of Lynching, 1889–1918*. Using the inarguable language of statistics, the book chronicled the lynchings of more than three thousand people. Some of the victims were white, but the majority were black. Most of the lynchings occurred in the Southern states. In an introduction to a 1969 reprint of the book, the NAACP's director, Roy Wilkins, wrote about that dark time: "There was only fear and helplessness...The president was silent. The U.S. Supreme Court could not hear. There was nowhere to turn." Wilkins went on to list some of the offenses that triggered the lynching of black people. They included such "crimes" as using offensive language or disagreeing with a white man.

STOPPED IN THE SENATE

President Woodrow Wilson officially condemned lynching in 1918, but a presidential proclamation was not sufficient to stop the tide of hatred. Things got even worse in the summer of 1919, when race riots occurred in dozens of cities across the country. James Weldon Johnson, a black activist and early leader of the NAACP, witnessed the bloodshed and called it the "Red Summer."

In the wake of this violence, the NAACP stepped up its efforts to stop lynching. One of the association's members, Walter White, traveled to the South to investigate. White had

National Guardsmen are called out to quell race riots in Chicago, Illinois, in July 1919.

African American blood, but his appearance, with light hair and blue eyes, allowed him to pass for white—up to a point. When word got around that a "white Negro" was undercover in Arkansas, White had to leave town before the violence caught up with him as well.

In 1918, Missouri congressman Leonidas Dyer proposed an anti-lynching law. Lynching was already illegal, but many state and local authorities, especially in the South, turned a blind eye to the crime. The Dyer bill would have made lynching a federal crime. That would allow the federal government to prosecute if the states did not do so. The bill sat in Congress for years. Although the House of Representatives passed it overwhelmingly, it was repeatedly blocked in the Senate by Southern legislators.

This pattern was to be repeated in the coming decades. Another bill failed in 1934 when, again, Southern senators blocked its passage. Some states passed anti-lynching laws, but the national government never did. The NAACP finally abandoned its efforts in the late 1940s, when lynching had become less common and the association decided that other issues facing black citizens needed more attention. However, the NAACP's work had helped publicize the lynching problem and sway public opinion against it.

SWEET SUCCESS

After World War I, unemployment was a problem. With thousands of men returning to America, competition for jobs was fierce. Many whites were angry that blacks were trying to fill some of the positions they felt should be given to whites. Also as a result of the war, a black migration had begun. The war had created a need for more industrial workers. Many African Americans left their homes in the rural South and began to move into Northern cities, where they hoped to find better jobs and schools and less outright racism. The North was more tolerant than the South, but the influx of blacks threatened to upset the economic and social balance. It caused problems there, too.

The NAACP took on a major legal battle in 1925–26 with the case of Ossian Sweet. Sweet, an African American physician, had moved into a white neighborhood in Detroit, Michigan. When a white mob attacked his home one night, Sweet and several of his family members and friends fought back. A white man was killed during the struggle. The NAACP investigated the incident and decided to help. Although the organization had limited resources, its leaders thought that the Sweet case was worth taking on. If they won, it would help the cause of blacks everywhere.

The NAACP hired a famous and talented lawyer, Clarence Darrow, to argue the Sweet case. In the end, Darrow convinced an all-white jury to find Sweet's brother Henry, who faced

The legal efforts of the NAACP helped African American Ossian Sweet defend the right to protect himself and his home. His Detroit, Michigan, house is now a historic landmark.

the most severe charges, innocent. The charges against the other defendants were dropped. This victory was an important milestone for the NAACP. It showed its members that the organization's focus was not solely on philosophical issues but on real problems—such as the right to defend one's home— that African Americans faced on a daily basis.

THE HARLEM RENAISSANCE

Fighting against violence and discrimination, particularly in the legal arena, was one strategy of the NAACP. But the organization also recognized the importance of empowering blacks in other ways. In 1925, an NAACP press release listed the organization's goals. The headings included segregation, legal defense, lynching, and discrimination.

KEEP TALKING

When senators believe strongly in a topic, they can talk for a long time! In the Senate, as long as one person is talking, no one else can. A filibuster is a long speech that allows a senator to hold the floor and prevent a particular issue from coming to a vote. If the senator can drag things out, a bill may expire before the whole Senate can vote on it.

In 1917, a new Senate rule introduced "cloture." Under this rule, a two-thirds majority could override a filibuster. Still, it's tough to do. Filibusters have prevented many controversial bills from coming to a vote. Senators filibustered to stop anti-lynching bills, and in 1964, they filibustered for fifty-seven days to try to stop an important civil rights bill. It eventually passed anyway, when cloture was enacted.

Another category was "cultural and artistic development of the Negro."

Many within the NAACP championed the idea of a New Negro Movement. The movement focused on art, music, and culture as a way to celebrate black heritage and achievements, and to bring new respect to African Americans. Much of the activity was centered in Harlem in New York City, where many black artists lived. The movement gave birth to such cultural icons as authors Langston Hughes and Zora Neale Hurston and jazz musicians Fats Waller

Famous musician Duke Ellington *(center)* is shown in a 1935 photo with members of his jazz trio. The Harlem Renaissance of the 1920s and 1930s nurtured black artists, musicians, and writers.

and Duke Ellington. W. E. B. Du Bois promoted work by black artists in *The Crisis* magazine.

As with any cultural movement, however, there was controversy. Du Bois and others sometimes criticized black artists when they showed African Americans in menial or base roles. "All art is propaganda," Du Bois said in a 1926 speech, arguing that African American artists had a responsibility to portray blacks in a positive light.

Of course, artists will do what they want, and the movement flourished in spite of—or perhaps because of—some of the controversies. Whatever the criticisms, the Harlem Renaissance affirmed the talents of blacks. The works of literature, art, and music that they produced were just as impressive as those of white artists. The Harlem Renaissance flowered in the 1920s and thrived for a few glorious years. But then the stock market crashed in 1929, the Great Depression of the 1930s set in, and all Americans—black and white—faced trouble.

Chapter 3

FIGHTING WITH THE LAW

The NAACP used legal action as one of its main ways to fight discrimination. The laws of the land protected blacks in theory, but the sad truth was that racism did not stop at the courtroom door. Even with a strong case, African Americans could lose if the judge or jury who heard the case believed that blacks did not deserve the same rights as whites.

BUILDING POLITICAL MUSCLE

The NAACP believed that Judge John J. Parker was one such person. When President Herbert Hoover nominated him to join the Supreme Court in 1930, the NAACP protested. In a political speech, Parker had made comments objecting to blacks being allowed to vote or participate in politics. While Parker's statements were fairly usual for Southern politicians of the time, the NAACP disagreed. Parker may have believed blacks had no place in the political process, but African Americans believed otherwise. They were about to demonstrate how involved they could be.

Walter White was the executive secretary of the NAACP from 1931 to 1955. He helped build the NAACP's formidable legal team, which would lay the foundation for equal rights for African Americans.

Walter White led the NAACP's campaign to block Parker's confirmation. The association reached out to its many members and urged them to contact their senators to state their opposition. Parker had other critics, too. In several lawsuits, he had ruled against labor unions having any power. Many people objected to that. As the campaign achieved a higher profile, Parker's support dwindled. Eventually, due to a combination of race and labor issues, his nomination was rejected in the Senate.

This event was particularly notable for the NAACP. It had successfully staged a grassroots effort and achieved results. The organization had effectively reached out to its rank-and-file members to enlighten them about the issue and gain their support. The NAACP's role in Parker's defeat encouraged White. Keeping racist judges from being appointed, or racist politicians from being elected, would help the NAACP's cause tremendously. White turned his attention to campaigning against other political candidates that the NAACP believed would hurt African Americans' progress. Over the next five years, the NAACP helped defeat several candidates it considered racist and rallied its members to support pro-black politicians.

LOOKING FOR FIRMER GROUND

African Americans had gained some political ground in the early 1930s, but everyday issues were more pressing for most people. The Great Depression dragged on, digging deeper into the wallets of Americans. At a 1933 meeting, NAACP leaders identified economic pressure as the primary struggle facing African Americans. Not only did the Depression result in fewer jobs overall, but there was tension between blacks and whites about who should receive those jobs. There was also tension between workers and employers about how black employees should be treated.

As during other times of national trouble, the Depression caused a shift in the country's demographics. Thousands of blacks moved to Northern cities, hoping to find better jobs, but there weren't enough to go around. Cities became flooded with unemployed people. Ghettos formed, filled with poor blacks who were becoming more and more desperate.

The South had its own problems. In 1932, a young NAACP worker named Roy Wilkins traveled to Mississippi and disguised himself as a poor laborer. He put his life in danger as he documented the situation of blacks working for the government's War Department on a flood control project. The working conditions were horrid, and the pay was dismal. As a result of the investigation, the NAACP publicized the situation. The next year, the black laborers received more money and shorter hours.

Members of the NAACP gathered in Cleveland, Ohio, for the organization's twentieth annual meeting in 1929. The group devoted itself to changing social and economic policies to be fair to blacks.

By the late 1930s, World War II had begun in Europe. In 1941, the United States joined the effort to defeat Germany's Adolf Hitler and his oppressive government. American forces needed all the help they could get, yet the conditions for black soldiers had not really improved since World War I. The NAACP lobbied President Franklin D. Roosevelt to allow blacks to work in the defense industry, which was mushrooming due to the war. Roosevelt hesitated. To publicize the cause, the association planned a march in Washington, D.C., in 1941. Under the threat of a public relations disaster, Roosevelt

relented. He issued an executive order barring discrimination in the government's defense industries.

GETTING OUT THE VOTE

From its earliest days, one of the NAACP's goals was to gain blacks equal access at the polls. Blacks were constitutionally guaranteed the right to vote, but many were not able to exercise it. Many rules and laws were in place to keep blacks away from the polls. Sometimes they were required to pass literacy tests. Other times they were charged a poll tax, or fee, in order to vote, and many could not afford to pay it. Hostility and intimidation by white supremacists kept many away from

MY COUNTRY, 'TIS OF THEE...

"...Sweet Land of Liberty." Those were the words that Marian Anderson sang on Easter Sunday, 1939. But was it truly a land of liberty? Anderson, a famous concert singer, was performing in front of the Lincoln Memorial in Washington, D.C., because she had been denied the opportunity to sing at the city's Constitution Hall. The Daughters of the American Revolution (DAR), which owned Constitution Hall, barred Anderson from singing there because she was black. The NAACP protested, but the DAR would not back

History was made on Easter Sunday in 1939, when African American singer Marian Anderson stood on the steps of the Lincoln Memorial and sang to an audience of thousands.

down. Anderson switched venues—and made history. Her performance was hailed as a stand against racism. The first lady, Eleanor Roosevelt, resigned her membership in the DAR in protest. The president himself, Franklin Roosevelt, just wanted to hear the famous singer. He reportedly said, "I don't care if she sings from the top of the Washington Monument, as long as she sings."

the polls out of fear. In the Southern states especially, few eligible blacks were even registered to vote. The NAACP worked for decades to fight against these trends.

Even in places where blacks faced fewer obstacles to voting, the NAACP had to work to convince African Americans that they should vote. Many blacks believed that politics did not really concern them and that their votes would not make a difference. However, the NAACP believed that change would come from a collection of voices raised together in the form of voting.

One victory came when the NAACP successfully challenged a 1923 Texas law that said only whites could vote in the Democratic primary. The Supreme Court ruled that this was unconstitutional. However, Texas politicians did not want blacks to vote in the primary. They passed new legislation that characterized the Democratic Party as a private organization. That would put it out of government control. It could decide for itself who was allowed to vote. African Americans cried foul, and another series of legal challenges followed. Finally, in 1944, the Supreme Court ruled that primaries were an integral part of the election process and that blacks must be included.

In the 1940s, '50s, and '60s, NAACP workers stayed busy registering black voters, often in the face of violence. Between 1940 and 1952, the number of registered black voters increased eightfold, representing approximately a quarter of the eligible black population. Just as its theme song proclaimed, the NAACP was working to "Lift Ev'ry Voice."

SETTING A PRECEDENT

Walter White, who took the helm of the NAACP in 1931 and led the organization until 1955, believed the organization's strength came from mounting legal challenges. The NAACP chose education as its next major battleground. Perhaps nowhere was segregation and discrimination more widespread, or more damaging, than in schools. In 1930, the NAACP hired a lawyer, Nathan Margold, to look into the situation. Margold wrote a report documenting the extent of the problem. He recommended a legal strategy that the NAACP could use to challenge the constitutionality of segregated public schools.

However, these were grand ambitions for an organization that did not have very much money and was still building its overall influence. The head of the NAACP's legal committee, Charles Hamilton Houston, worried that it could not immediately accomplish something as far-reaching as ending all segregation in public schools. Instead, he crafted another legal strategy. His plan was to try cases of discrimination in universities and then use the victories to establish a series of legal precedents. Over time, these would chip away at the "separate but equal" concept and pave the way to abolishing segregation in elementary and high schools.

Lloyd Gaines was a young African American who wanted to attend law school at the University of Missouri. When the university denied him entrance, the NAACP successfully sued on his behalf.

Houston's strategy proved brilliant. With the help of Thurgood Marshall, one of his most promising students from his days at Howard University School of Law, Houston's legal team began a prolonged attack. In the coming decades, a string of cases would allow the NAACP to prove that the educational opportunities of black and white students were not equal.

In Missouri in the 1930s, no state law schools admitted black students. As a result, student Lloyd Gaines was denied admission to the University of Missouri's law school. Instead, the university offered to pay for him to attend law school in another state. The NAACP helped with Gaines's lawsuit, arguing that sending him to an out-of-state school was not acceptable. In *Missouri ex. rel. Gaines v. Canada* (1938), the Supreme Court ruled that the university had a choice: Build another, equal law facility for blacks, or let Gaines into the existing law school.

Graduate schools in Texas and Oklahoma faced similar suits in 1950. The schools offered to create programs just for blacks, keeping them separate from white students. In *Sweatt v. Painter* and *McLaurin v. Oklahoma State Regents*, the NAACP successfully argued that such an option was not equal. It would isolate black students from the rest of the student body, and deny them important interaction that contributed to their education. The U.S. Supreme Court agreed and required the two states to admit black students to their graduate schools.

Slowly, states that had previously barred black students from their graduate programs began to admit them. It might have been integration granted unwillingly, but at least it was a start.

Chapter 4

THE FIGHT FOR FREEDOM

By the close of the 1940s, the NAACP was facing trouble. Dues had doubled—to $2 a year—but membership was plummeting. In 1948, there were just over half as many members as there had been a few years earlier at the end of World War II. Some African Americans felt the NAACP concentrated too much on fighting philosophical and legal battles that didn't make a real difference in people's lives. But the NAACP was laying the groundwork for huge changes, and within the next decade, those changes would start to make a difference.

TO SECURE THESE RIGHTS

In 1947, the NAACP issued a report that showed how blacks suffered from injustices and how the U.S. government failed to protect their rights. Only a week later, the government came out with its own report, *To Secure These Rights*, which took a comprehensive look at the lives of black Americans. It documented how race affected all kinds of issues, from education to employment, housing to health care—all the issues that concerned the NAACP.

The report launched a national debate about civil rights. In 1948, President Harry Truman officially came out in support of civil rights for blacks, and he banned discrimination within the federal government. While this was a step forward, it did not have a huge effect, since most blacks did not work for the government. Discrimination was still widespread. The places where racism plagued African Americans went far beyond federal offices.

In 1953, the NAACP launched its "Fight for Freedom" campaign. The movement aimed to end segregation and discrimination against blacks within a decade—by 1963, the one hundredth anniversary of Lincoln's issuance of the Emancipation Proclamation.

One constant battleground was public transportation. Blacks and whites were forced to sit in different sections on public buses and trains. If there weren't enough seats, blacks were expected to stand so that whites could sit. In 1944, Irene Morgan, who was black, refused to give up her seat for a white person on a bus in Virginia. Morgan was arrested, but in the trials that followed, the NAACP proved that she had done nothing wrong. The bus had been headed to Maryland, and it would cross state lines. In *Morgan v. Virginia* (1946), the NAACP successfully argued to the Supreme Court that the Virginia law interfered with interstate commerce and could not be enforced. The victory was only a small slice of success, to be sure, because it covered only interstate buses and trains. Nevertheless, it was a step forward for civil rights.

A decade later, when Rosa Parks refused to yield her seat to a white person in Montgomery, Alabama, the foundation had been laid. Parks's case caused a sensation in Alabama. The city's black population, led by Dr. Martin Luther King Jr.,

Thousands of African Americans walk to work during the 1956 bus boycott in Montgomery, Alabama. The system did not allow blacks to ride the buses under the same conditions as whites.

rallied to her cause. They boycotted the buses in Montgomery for more than a year. Meanwhile, the NAACP fought for Parks in the legal arena. The NAACP's lawyers feared Parks's case could get bogged down in the Alabama courts, so the legal team looked for a different approach. First, it found several similar instances of discrimination against black people on buses. It combined them into a class-action suit that went straight to federal court and bypassed the state courts altogether. It worked: the U.S. Supreme Court ruled in *Browder v. Gayle* (1956) that bus segregation in Alabama was unconstitutional. Three days after the Court's decision, the city of Montgomery was forced to desegregate its buses. Black people could ride the bus under the same conditions as whites.

A MAJOR VICTORY

According to historian Patricia Sullivan, author of the book *Lift Every Voice*, NAACP leader Roy Wilkins stated in a 1951 speech, "More damage…has been done to [black youth] by the denial of equal opportunity in education than by all the lynching mobs in our history." This statement laid bare the reality. Separate was not equal, and it never could be.

In the 1930s and on up to 1950, the NAACP's lawyers had won a string of victories on the issue of segregated education, proving that separate facilities and programs were not good enough. The Supreme Court had agreed with the NAACP's argument that "qualities incapable of objective measurement" factored into the definition of "equal." In other words, equality was about more than dishes and dorm rooms. It was about whom blacks could interact with on a daily basis and how they were treated. Steadily, the NAACP had demonstrated that there could be no equality of educational opportunity until blacks were permitted to freely associate and intermingle with whites. The antiquated *Plessy v. Ferguson* ruling—with its idea of "separate but equal"—had not been struck down yet, but it was standing on shakier ground. The pressure of new precedents had pushed it to the breaking point, and the NAACP's lead attorney, Thurgood Marshall, knew it.

As Charles Hamilton Houston's successor, Marshall had managed the organization's legal strategy since 1938, and he was now ready to go for the big prize. According to the National Park Service, Marshall announced in a 1950 meeting, "We are going to insist on non-segregation in American public education from top to bottom—from law school to kindergarten." The first test came later that year, when several families in South Carolina filed suit against their local school district, protesting segregation. The NAACP lost the case in federal district court, but it decided to appeal to the U.S. Supreme Court.

Another important case began in 1951 in Topeka, Kansas. Linda Brown, the young daughter of Reverend Oliver Brown, and several other African American children were denied the right to attend white elementary schools in their own neighborhoods. Instead, they had to travel to attend one of the city's four black schools. The NAACP took the case to a panel of federal judges. As had happened in previous cases, the panel ruled that the schools were equal, meeting the standard of the *Plessy v. Ferguson* ruling. However, one of the judges, Walter Huxman, pointed out that segregation was having a negative effect on black students.

According to the book *Jim Crow's Children* by Peter Irons, Huxman later said the panel did not like having to decide

Linda Brown, an African American elementary student in Kansas, sits in her all-black classroom. Later, she became the face of a historic lawsuit that struck down segregated schools.

in favor of segregation. "If it weren't for *Plessy v. Ferguson*, we surely would have found the law unconstitutional," the judge said. "But there was no way around it—the Supreme Court would have to overrule itself."

The stage was set, and the children in Kansas and South Carolina were not alone. Children in Virginia faced the same problem. So did ones in Delaware and Washington, D.C. In fact, the situation, with a few variations, was repeated nationwide. More and more black families were demanding justice. The Supreme Court decided to hear five key cases of school

Thurgood Marshall, lead lawyer for the NAACP, stands outside the U.S. Supreme Court building in 1955. Marshall successfully argued *Brown v. Board of Education*, which outlawed segregation in public schools.

segregation filed by the NAACP, beginning in December 1952. The cases were bundled together and heard under the name *Oliver Brown, et al. v. the Board of Education of Topeka, et al.* This case would become a landmark in civil rights and one of the most famous Supreme Court cases in American history, best known as *Brown v. Board of Education.*

The legal system tends to move slowly, but by May 1954, the Supreme Court had made its decision. In a unanimous vote, it ruled that segregation was unconstitutional. Separate was not equal. *Plessy v. Ferguson* was finally dead, and the NAACP had won the legal fight it had launched nearly twenty-five years earlier.

NOT OVER YET

The moral battle, however, was still being fought, especially in the South. Before the Supreme Court even made its ruling, school districts in the South were scheming to evade deseg-regation. The governor of South Carolina said that if the Court ruled in favor of integration, he would close the state's schools and convert them to a private system. Furthermore, despite the NAACP's urging, the Supreme Court had not dic-tated how or when the school districts had to change. With no deadline, many school districts stalled in desegregation actions or relied on other methods to keep segregation in place. One method was "freedom of choice." In theory, this let parents enroll their students in the school that they pre-ferred. In practice, however, white students tended not to choose schools that were largely black, and many black stu-dents did not choose white schools out of fear.

THE LITTLE ROCK NINE

Resistance to desegregation turned ugly in 1957. In Little Rock, Arkansas, NAACP leader Daisy Bates helped nine black students enroll in the previously all-white Central High School. But when the time came for class, the students were prevented from entering. Tensions escalated as the situation gained national attention. Someone threw a rock through the window at Bates's home. A note attached to it read, "Stone this time. Dynamite next." But Bates didn't back down. She continued to help the students, who became known as the Little Rock Nine, in their struggle. Eventually, President Dwight Eisenhower had to send federal troops to enforce integration, and the students went to school.

Nine African American students in Little Rock, Arkansas, integrated into an all-white high school in 1957. Federal troops were called in to protect them from violence.

Some states went after the NAACP itself. In the mid-1950s, integration was still more of a concept than a reality. The government did not directly enforce integration, and most black families had neither the money nor the will to fight the system by themselves. Instead, they relied on the money, influence, and expertise of the NAACP. If states could cut off their citizens from the one organization equipped to help them, they could keep segregation in place. Thus, several states attacked the association and charged it with operating illegally. They made the NAACP pay fees that other organizations did not, and prohibited city and state employees from becoming members. In Alabama, where resistance to integration was extreme, the NAACP was banned until 1964.

Squeezed by white racism, the NAACP faced declining membership in the Southern states during this difficult time. It held on, though, and by the 1960s, the association's determination would pay off in more victories.

Chapter 5

CHASING THE DREAM

T he NAACP hoped education would be the first major breakthrough against a racist system in general, but its members knew that it wasn't just schools at issue. It was restaurants and hotels, museums and department stores, bowling alleys and skating rinks. There was no equality on two sides of a color line. The barrier had to come down—everywhere.

TAKING A "CRUMB"

In 1957, a long-awaited civil rights bill came before Congress. The bill provided for the establishment of a civil rights commission. It ordered the federal government to protect voting rights and gave the government the power to intervene when constitutional rights were being violated. However, the bill also said that violators could be tried only before a jury. That meant that in the South, it would be primarily whites sitting in judgment on other whites, and this would probably not result in any convictions. Within the NAACP, opinions were sharply divided. Many opposed supporting the watered-down bill, which would do little to improve the situation of black citizens.

Others argued that the bill might be weak, but it was a start. And they had to start somewhere.

NAACP executive secretary Roy Wilkins opted to have the association support the bill. According to the book *Freedom's Sword* by Gilbert Jonas, he said later that he kept in mind a piece of advice to "never…turn your back on a crumb." Wilkins wrote in his autobiography, "The crumb of 1957 had to come before the civil rights acts that followed." Congress passed the bill even though South Carolina Senator Strom Thurmond filibustered for more than twenty-four hours to try to stop it. In the following years, blacks in America increasingly demanded their equal rights, and the 1957 law helped pave the way.

Roy Wilkins, a longtime worker for the NAACP, took over as leader of the organization in 1955. He would be in charge during the tumultuous civil rights era of the 1950s and 1960s.

DIRECT ACTION

The NAACP had chosen to fight primarily through legal challenges, but by the 1960s, another approach was gaining ground: direct action. On February 1, 1960, a group of four black college students went to a lunch counter at a Woolworth's store in Greensboro, North Carolina. They refused to leave despite the hostility of the police and other white customers. A larger group of black students returned the next day. The national press pounced on the story. A wave of similar sit-ins spread throughout the South.

As the civil rights movement gained momentum, more organizations formed to unite black citizens against a white stronghold. Perhaps the most famous was the Southern Christian Leadership Conference (SCLC), founded in 1957 following the Montgomery bus boycott and led by Dr. Martin Luther King Jr. Others included the Congress of Racial Equality (CORE), established in 1942; the Student Nonviolent Coordinating Committee (SNCC), founded in 1960; and the Black Panthers, formed in 1966. These organizations chose

College students sit at a lunch counter in Little Rock, Arkansas, in 1962, to protest the restaurant's refusal to serve blacks. Similar demonstrations took place across the country.

to actively demonstrate against discrimination by staging marches, sit-ins, and other emotionally charged events.

However, the confrontational type of direct action was a style embraced more by younger activists, not the NAACP as a whole. The organization worked to find common ground with its fellow protesters. Roy Wilkins welcomed the visibility that direct action could bring. The acts were emotional and personal. They generated sympathy—or at least awareness—on the national stage. Still, Wilkins believed that only the muscle and perseverance of the NAACP would ultimately bring real change. In addition, he did not want resources to be wasted on unsuccessful efforts. Though the Montgomery bus boycott had succeeded in its goal, Wilkins worried that other efforts, in which the situation was not as sympathetic to blacks, might fail. In that case, plans could backfire because they could serve to strengthen the racist attitudes of whites. Despite the immediate attention that some other civil rights organizations brought to the larger fight, Wilkins believed that the NAACP's long track record, especially in legal battles, was an even greater weapon.

BLACK POWER

Of the civil rights organizations that campaigned for equal rights in the 1960s, the NAACP was by far the largest and most powerful. Each had a slightly different style, but it was the NAACP that had the broadest membership base and the most expertise. For one thing, the NAACP had the largest numbers, with almost four hundred thousand members in 1961. With some 1,300 units, including adults, youths, and students, the NAACP was in every corner of America.

This enabled it to muster reliable support on a national level. Also, in dealing with the white establishment, the association had a lot of influence. However, some supporters of direct action felt that the NAACP was too conservative. As the civil rights movement became more heated in the 1960s, some activists became even more militant.

Stokely Carmichael was an influential black activist who had joined both CORE and SNCC (popularly pronounced "snick"). He advocated peaceful methods at first but became increasingly frustrated and angry about the discrimination to which blacks were subjected. After an activist was attacked during a protest march in 1966, Carmichael made an impassioned speech. "We been saying 'freedom' for six years," he said, according to his obituary in the *New York Times*. "What we are going to start saying now is 'black power!'"

Pictured here in 1967, Stokely Carmichael was an activist who favored Black Power, which supported using any means necessary—including violence—in support of African American rights.

The Black Power movement supported doing whatever was necessary to further the cause. Unlike the NAACP's or Dr. King's legendary peaceful approaches, proponents of

Black Power would resort to violence when they thought it was needed to make a point.

Within the Black Power movement was another idea: black separatism. Followers of this philosophy believed that black people should not accept integration with whites. Instead, they supported a position of separatism, in which black people stuck together and celebrated their achievements apart from whites. The whole notion of being "separate" contradicted what the NAACP had advocated for decades. NAACP president Roy Wilkins forcefully rejected the idea of Black Power, which he characterized as "anti-white power." "[It] is a reverse Mississippi, a reverse Hitler, a reverse Ku Klux Klan. Black Power…can mean in the end only black death," he said according to Yvonne Ryan, author of the book *Roy Wilkins: The Quiet Revolutionary and the NAACP*. It wasn't just about how whites treated blacks; it was about how blacks treated whites as well. The NAACP's position was that it opposed racism in all forms.

LANDMARK LEGISLATION

In 1963, President John F. Kennedy pressed Congress to pass a civil rights bill that was clear, comprehensive, and strong. The bill was moving through the House of Representatives when Kennedy was assassinated on November 22 of that year. Not only was his death a national tragedy, but it was also a political blow to the bill. Southern conservatives were very much opposed to it. The NAACP faced months of trying to work through the roadblocks that the bill's opponents threw up, but the association held firm. One NAACP worker, Clarence Mitchell, spent so much time talking to legislators that he became unofficially known as "the 101st senator."

President Lyndon B. Johnson shakes hands with African American leader Dr. Martin Luther King Jr. at the signing of the Civil Rights Act in 1964.

Fortunately, Kennedy's successor, President Lyndon Johnson, also supported the bill. It passed in the House but faced extraordinary opposition in the Senate, where Southern senators filibustered for a record fifty-seven days to keep it from coming to a vote. However, the time was finally right. On June 10, 1964, for the first time in Senate history, a filibuster against a civil rights bill was officially ended through a vote for cloture, and the legislation was able to pass. On July 2, 1964, the House voted to adopt the Senate version of the bill, and President Johnson signed it into law.

THE MARCH ON WASHINGTON

In 1963, the NAACP became involved with a plan to march on Washington. The organization agreed to contribute money and organizational help as several civil rights groups banded together to plan the event. The march, held on August 28, 1963, brought together more than 250,000 people, both white and black, who gathered in front of the Lincoln Memorial. There, they listened to speeches that urged the government to finally authorize a civil rights bill that would protect blacks—and all Americans—equally. It was at this march that Dr. Martin Luther King Jr. delivered his "I Have a Dream" speech. With its simple and eloquent plea for equality and fairness, it became one of the most famous speeches in American history.

There was, however, a significant omission in the Civil Rights Act of 1964. The right of black citizens to vote was not sufficiently protected. Thus, almost immediately after the law passed, the NAACP focused its efforts on the next struggle. In the South, black citizens were effectively being denied the right to vote by being forced to take difficult literacy tests. Supposedly, these tests proved citizens were worthy of casting a vote. However, whites, in general, were not required to pass the tests. Tensions mounted as blacks were refused the right to register to vote, and violence escalated. Some blacks who demanded their rights were killed. So were some courageous white people who dared to stand with them.

NAACP lobbyists, now very familiar with the political landscape in Washington, D.C., appealed for justice in the way that they knew best: advocating a law. The resulting Voting Rights Act of 1965 made it illegal for states to discriminate against people of any race in voting practices. It eliminated the use of literacy tests as a condition of voting nationwide. To make the law stick, states that Congress believed to have the greatest potential for discrimination were required to submit their voting rules to be approved by the federal government. In addition to helping pass the new law, the NAACP and other civil rights organizations cooperated on the Voter Education Project, which was designed to register more African American voters.

Chapter 6

STRUGGLES OLD AND NEW

Duruing the 1960s, the NAACP's work had helped pass three major pieces of legislation: the Civil Rights Act (1964), the Voting Rights Act (1965), and the Fair Housing Act (1968). Yet there was still a major arena where blacks were not treated equally: the workplace.

WORKING FOR CHANGE

The NAACP had been working to open up job opportunities for African Americans for decades. It had pressured the federal government to open the doors of the military and treat black workers with decency and respect. In the 1950s, the NAACP teamed up with several labor unions, hoping to gain support for civil rights legislation. However, the support tended to be limited to the upper management of the unions. Within the rank and file, blatantly racist practices still punished black workers.

Herbert Hill, the labor secretary of the NAACP, worked for twenty-five years to right these wrongs. The NAACP was involved in a notable case in 1962 against the New York chapter of the International Ladies' Garment Workers' Union (ILGWU). The ILGWU had cooperated with the NAACP on desegregation efforts in other parts of the country. Hill was risking his professional reputation to take them on, but he felt strongly that the New York chapter discriminated against blacks. Eventually Hill won the case, forcing the ILGWU to offer blacks jobs that previously had gone only to whites.

A few years later, Hill had another weapon at his disposal. The Civil Rights Act of 1964 included a clause called Title VII. It prohibited employers from discriminating against blacks or other people of color based on their race. (It also prohibited discrimination on the basis of gender or religion.) This clause gave blacks a concrete basis on which to file suit over unfair labor practices, if necessary.

In 1971, the NAACP participated in another landmark case. In *Griggs v. Duke Power*, NAACP lead lawyer Jack Greenberg went to the Supreme Court on behalf of thirteen African American employees of Duke Power in North Carolina. He successfully argued that the power company had unfairly discriminated against blacks by requiring them to pass tests for certain jobs, even when the jobs did not require the knowledge for which they were being tested.

CREATING AN IMAGE

Hill also worked with the entertainment industry to try to end racial bias in that field. Ever since the 1915 film *Birth of a Nation*, the NAACP had tried to improve how African Americans were portrayed in movies and on TV. It also worked to open the doors to jobs in the entertainment industry. Throughout the first half of the century, there were few roles for blacks in mainstream

Kerry Washington receives the award for Outstanding Actress in a Drama Series at the NAACP's 2013 Image Awards. Washington has received several Image Awards during her career.

entertainment. Of the ones that existed, most showed blacks in negative or subservient roles. A few black filmmakers made movies that starred African Americans and portrayed them as smart and successful, but these films were not usually distributed to wide audiences.

NAACP leaders understood from the start that popular media had a huge influence on how blacks were perceived. In 1942, Walter White established an NAACP committee to track how blacks were being portrayed in the entertainment industry—and what it found wasn't positive. Books and art from the Harlem Renaissance had helped promote a positive image of blacks, but movies and television had an even wider reach. They had a profound impact on the larger American public. In 1966, the NAACP protested against the *Amos 'n Andy Show,* complaining of racial stereotyping, and succeeded in getting it taken off the air.

The problem wasn't limited to fiction: in 1955, an NAACP field worker named Medgar Evers filed a complaint against a Mississippi television station of racial bias in its news reporting. The station subsequently lost its broadcasting license. (Evers was later assassinated in conjunction with his work for the NAACP.)

In 1967, the Beverly Hills-Hollywood branch of the NAACP launched the Image Awards. These were awarded to black performers, writers, directors, and producers who had made significant achievements in the field and whose work had improved the image of African Americans. The Image Awards are still given out each year.

STEERING A NEW COURSE

The NAACP had made huge advances for African Americans in its decades of work, yet the association still faced issues. In the 1970s, bankruptcy threatened as membership dropped. The organization faced criticism from more militant groups about being irrelevant.

The 1980s brought more problems when the administration of President Ronald Reagan cut funding and support to civil rights causes. In 1989, the Supreme Court made a number of decisions that the NAACP believed would have a negative effect on African Americans' rights. The association held a march to protest the Court's rulings, which would reduce affirmative action programs and make it more difficult for employees to fight back against unfair circumstances. Meanwhile, it publicized injustices and violence in South Africa, where the social system of apartheid oppressed the black population.

In the early 1990s, the organization faced more financial trouble. It was several million dollars in debt, and donations withered amid reports of the organization's chairman misusing its funds. There was also a shakeup among the leadership when the NAACP fired its executive director in 1994.

Chairman of the National Board of Directors Julian Bond *(left)* and president and CEO Kweisi Mfume *(right)* led the NAACP in the late 1990s and early 2000s. They appear at the NAACP's eighty-ninth annual convention in Atlanta, Georgia.

In addition to its internal troubles, the NAACP now had another hurdle. After the monumental legislative acts of the 1960s, the association struggled to rekindle the spirit of activism that had characterized it during its most productive years. Kweisi Mfume, president and CEO of the NAACP from 1996 to 2004, and Julian Bond, who was elected board chairman in 1998, took on that challenge. Part of their work involved revitalizing the NAACP's political reach and influence. In practice, this usually meant siding with Democrats, who tended to be more liberal.

ACT-SO

African American journalist Vernon Jarrett devoted his career to covering issues affecting blacks. In 1946, on his first day on the job at the *Chicago Defender*, he covered a race riot. In the following decades, he saw the many problems confronting blacks—especially young blacks. He later became the first African American syndicated columnist at the *Chicago Tribune*.

According to an article in the *Washington Post*, Jarrett wanted to help empower young people to overcome what he believed was a "smothering climate" that had low expectations of black students. In 1977, he founded the Afro-Academic, Cultural, Technical, and Scientific Olympics (ACT-SO). The program, sponsored by the NAACP, rewards African American youths who achieve in various fields. Students embark on a yearlong program to build their skills and then participate in an annual competition.

However, this led to problems within the NAACP's ranks. Mfume and Bond had deep differences about how the NAACP should assign its loyalties. In 2003, Mfume nominated Condoleezza Rice, National Security Advisor under President George W. Bush, to be honored with an NAACP Image Award. Bond opposed this choice. He was appalled at Mfume's desire to reach out to the Republican Party, which had long opposed many NAACP causes. In the end, Mfume left the NAACP.

The NAACP ran up against the Bush administration again when President Bush declined to speak at the association's national convention for several years in a row. Julian Bond had been outspokenly critical of many of Bush's choices in office. Bush recalled those slights and said that he had a "basically nonexistent" relationship with the organization, according to a 2004 article in the *Washington Post*. However, two years later, he did address NAACP members at its annual convention and seemed to try to mend the relationship.

INTO THE NEXT CENTURY

Today, the NAACP continues to work on behalf of African Americans and other minority groups. One cause that has a long history in the organization is voting rights. For decades, the NAACP has sponsored programs focused on registering people to vote—and then encouraging them to exercise that right during elections. Other efforts have included making sure minority populations are accurately

In 2009, the NAACP celebrated its one hundredth birthday, marking a century of working for causes such as civil rights, voting rights, fair housing, affirmative action, and equality in the workplace.

counted in the U.S. Census and are adequately represented in government.

The NAACP also works to raise awareness about environmental issues and health care. For example, it publicizes the fact that polluting factories are often situated in poor areas that have larger minority populations. On the work front, the association continues its efforts to achieve economic equality by promoting affirmative action and preparing African Americans to hold good jobs.

Blacks make up far more of the prison population than whites. So the NAACP also attempts to represent inmates, who often have few rights—and even fewer supporters. The first prison chapter of the NAACP opened in 1972, and for the last forty years, the organization has worked to protect the rights of blacks who are in prison and give them rights once they are released. It also advocates for law enforcement policies that better serve black communities.

In 2009, the NAACP celebrated its one hundredth anniversary. Just to exist for that long, amid countless attacks, is an accomplishment. Along the way, the NAACP has brought attention to conditions that African Americans face both in the United States and abroad. In the face of violence, it has remained peaceful. In the face of hostility, it has remained respectful. In the face of skepticism, it has remained vigilant. Through countless millions of hours of work—many on the part of volunteers—it has helped abolish discriminatory practices. Racism has always been a part of American history, but thanks in large part to the NAACP, one day it may only be a memory.

TIMELINE

1896 The Supreme Court, in the case of *Plessy v. Ferguson*, rules that public facilities can segregate whites and blacks, as long as the facilities are "separate but equal."

1905 W. E. B. Du Bois begins the Niagara Movement, a precursor to the NAACP.

1909 The NAACP is formed in New York City.

1918 The NAACP investigates the problem of lynching and publishes a book about it; the Dyer bill, an anti-lynching piece of legislation, is introduced in Congress.

1920s Black writers, artists, musicians, and scholars participate in the blossoming of African American culture known as the Harlem Renaissance.

1926 Clarence Darrow wins a major victory for the NAACP in defending Ossian Sweet and his family.

1929 The stock market crashes, triggering the Great Depression of the 1930s.

1930 The NAACP successfully blocks Judge John J. Parker from joining the Supreme Court.

1941 Under pressure from the NAACP, President Franklin D. Roosevelt bans discrimination in the government's defense industries.

1953 The NAACP launches its "Fight for Freedom" campaign, with the goal of ending segregation and discrimination in a decade.

1954 In a unanimous vote in *Brown v. Board of Education*, the Supreme Court overturns the "separate but equal" standard set in *Plessy v. Ferguson*. The Court rules that separate educational facilities based on race are unconstitutional.

1955 On December 1, Rosa Parks refuses to give up her seat on a bus in Montgomery, Alabama, leading to a yearlong boycott of the city's buses by African Americans.

1957 Congress passes the first civil rights law since just after the Civil War; President Dwight Eisenhower sends federal troops to enforce integration at Central High School in Little Rock, Arkansas.

1963 President John F. Kennedy proposes a civil rights act; in August, more than 250,000 people participate in the famous March on Washington to support it. Kennedy is assassinated in November.

1964 With substantial lobbying from the NAACP, Congress passes a major civil rights act giving African Americans more rights and protections under the law.

1965 Congress passes another landmark piece of legislation, the Voting Rights Act.

1967 The NAACP establishes the annual Image Awards to honor and recognize important African Americans.

1972 The NAACP establishes its first prison branch at the U.S. Penitentiary in Lewisburg, Pennsylvania.

1985 The NAACP organizes a march in New York City to protest violence in South Africa as a result of the country's apartheid system.

1989 The NAACP protests Supreme Court decisions it thought could adversely affect African Americans.

1990s Financial difficulties plague the NAACP in the first half of the decade, but it rebounds; the association stages a major voting drive for the 2000 presidential election.

2009 The NAACP celebrates its one hundredth anniversary.

2013 The NAACP sponsors two membership drives, "Remember Medgar" and "He is ME," to commemorate the fiftieth anniversary of the murder of NAACP activist Medgar Evers.

GLOSSARY

ABOLISH To put an end to something.

ACTIVIST A person who works for a cause.

AMEND To change.

APARTHEID A social system that separates blacks and whites and keeps the status of blacks inferior.

BOYCOTT To refuse to purchase or use something as a way of protesting.

CLASS-ACTION SUIT A lawsuit combining several people or similar cases in a common cause.

CONCESSION Something given up in order to reach an agreement or improve an overall situation.

DEMOGRAPHICS The statistical characteristics of a population, including categories such as race, age, gender, and income.

GHETTO A poor neighborhood often inhabited by minorities.

GRASSROOTS Originating in the efforts of ordinary people instead of top down, through the traditional channels of power.

INTERVENE To interrupt the progress of an action; to step in to change something.

LIBERAL Relating to or having views that support social and political change.

LYNCH To put to death, usually by hanging, without having legal grounds to do so.

MILITANT Using extreme, often confrontational, tactics in support of a cause.

MINSTREL A type of variety show in which white performers portrayed black people, usually negatively.

POLARIZED On opposite ends; sharply divided.

PRECEDENT A legal decision that is used as a standard for similar cases in the future.

PROPAGANDA The spreading of ideas, information, or rumor for a particular cause.

SEGREGATE To separate, usually by race.

SHARECROPPER A person, often black, who works for a landowner in return for a share of the crop, but usually at an economic disadvantage.

UNANIMOUS Having the agreement of all.

VOCATIONAL A type of education or training focusing on practical career skills.

American Civil Liberties Union (ACLU)
125 Broad Street, 18th Floor
New York, NY 10004
(212) 549-2500
Website: http://www.aclu.org
The American Civil Liberties Union provides legal
assistance to individuals facing violations of their
basic civil rights. It also champions the rights of
minority populations and other disadvantaged
groups.

Civil Rights Project at UCLA
8370 Math Sciences
Box 951521
Los Angeles, CA 90095-1521
Website: http://civilrightsproject.ucla.edu
The Civil Rights Project works to renew the civil rights movement by bridging the worlds of ideas and action and
promoting a deeper understanding of issues concerning
racial and ethnic equality.

Leadership Conference on Civil and Human Rights
1629 K Street NW, 10th Floor
Washington, DC 20006
(202) 466-3311
Website: http://www.civilrights.org
The Leadership Conference on Civil and Human Rights
was founded in 1950 by the leaders of several civil
rights groups to focus on lobbying for legislation to
ensure civil rights. It continues such work today.

National Association for the Advancement of Colored
    People (NAACP)
4805 Mt. Hope Drive
Baltimore, MD 21215
(410) 580-5777
Website: http://www.naacp.org
For more than a century, the NAACP has worked
    to gain equality for African Americans and other
    minorities in civil rights, economic justice, and
    other areas.

National Civil Rights Museum
450 Mulberry Street
Memphis, TN 38103
(901) 521-9699
Website: http://www.civilrightsmuseum.org
Located at the Lorraine Motel in Memphis, Tennessee,
    where Dr. Martin Luther King Jr. was assassinated, the
    museum has exhibits covering the African American
    experience and examining the impact of the American
    civil rights movement.

National Urban League
120 Wall Street
New York, NY 10005
(212) 558-5300
Website: http://nul.iamempowered.com
Founded in 1910, the National Urban League works to
    empower African Americans with economic equality and
    civil rights.

Smithsonian National Museum of African American History
    and Culture
14th Street and Constitution Avenue NW
Washington, DC 20001
(202) 633-1000
Website: http://nmaahc.si.edu
The Smithsonian's exhibit on African American History
    and Culture takes a comprehensive look at the roles of
    African Americans in the country's history. In 2015, the
    exhibit is expected to move to a permanent museum of
    its own.

WEBSITES

Due to the changing nature of Internet links, Rosen Publishing
has developed an online list of websites related to the subject
of this book. This site is updated regularly. Please use this link
to access the list:

http://www.rosenlinks.com/CCRM/NAACP

Barrett, Linda. *Miles to Go for Freedom: Segregation and Civil Rights in the Jim Crow Years.* New York, NY: Abrams Books for Young Readers, 2012.

Bjornlund, Lydia. *The Civil Rights Movement* (Understanding American History). San Diego, CA: ReferencePoint Press, 2013.

Bolden, Tonya. *W. E. B. Du Bois: A Twentieth Century Life* (Up Close). New York, NY: Viking, 2008.

Bowers, Rick. *Spies of Mississippi: The True Story of the Spy Network That Tried to Destroy the Civil Rights Movement.* Washington, DC: National Geographic Children's Books, 2010.

Capek, Michael, and Steven F. Lawson. *Civil Rights Movement* (Essential Library of Social Change). Minneapolis, MN: ABDO Publishing, 2014.

Cates, David, and Margalynne Armstrong. *Plessy v. Ferguson: Segregation and the Separate but Equal Policy* (Landmark Supreme Court Cases). Minneapolis, MN: ABDO Publishing, 2013.

Esty, Amos. *Plessy v. Ferguson* (The Civil Rights Movement). Greensboro, NC: Morgan Reynolds, 2012.

Feinstein, Stephen. *Inspiring African-American Civil Rights Leaders* (African-American Collective Biographies). Berkeley Heights, NJ: Enslow, 2013.

Herringshaw, DeAnn. *The Harlem Renaissance* (Essential Events). Minneapolis, MN: ABDO Publishing, 2012.

Hinton, KaaVonia. *Brown v. Board of Education of Topeka, Kansas, 1954* (Monumental Milestones). Hockessin, DE: Mitchell Lane Publishers, 2010.

Johnson, Robin. *March on Washington.* New York, NY: Crabtree Publishing, 2013.

Lyndon, Dan. *Civil Rights and Equality* (Black History). London, England: Franklin Watts, 2013.

Magoon, Kekla. *Today the World Is Watching You: The Little Rock Nine and the Fight for School Integration, 1957* (Civil Rights Struggles Around the World). Minneapolis, MN: Twenty-First Century Books, 2011.

NAACP and *The Crisis* Publishing Co. *NAACP: Celebrating a Century: 100 Years in Pictures.* Layton, UT: Gibbs Smith, 2009.

Nathan, Amy. *Round and Round Together: Taking a Merry-Go-Round Ride into the Civil Rights Movement.* Philadelphia, PA: Paul Dry Books, 2011.

Starks, Glenn L., and F. Erik Brooks. *Thurgood Marshall: A Biography* (Greenwood Biographies). Westport, CT: Greenwood Publishing, 2012.

BIBLIOGRAPHY

Allen, Mike. "Bush Criticizes NAACP's Leadership." *Washington Post*, July 10, 2004. Retrieved December 7, 2013 (http://www.washingtonpost.com/wp-dyn/articles/A40255 -2004Jul10.html).

Berg, Manfred. *The Ticket to Freedom: The NAACP and the Struggle for Black Political Integration.* Gainesville, FL: University Press of Florida, 2005.

Bernstein, Patricia. *The First Waco Horror: The Lynching of Jesse Washington and the Rise of the NAACP.* College Station, TX: Texas A&M University Press, 2005.

Educational Broadcasting Corporation. "The Rise and Fall of Jim Crow." PBS.org, 2002. Retrieved June 22, 2013 (http://www.pbs.org/wnet/jimcrow/stories_events.html).

Finch, Minnie. *The NAACP: Its Fight for Justice.* Metuchen, NJ: The Scarecrow Press, 1981.

Goings, Kenneth W. *The NAACP Comes of Age: The Defeat of Judge John J. Parker.* Bloomington, IN: Indiana University Press, 1990.

Hughes, Langston. *Fight for Freedom: The Story of the NAACP.* New York, NY: W. W. Norton and Company, 1962.

Irons, Peter H. *Jim Crow's Children: The Broken Promise of the Brown Decision.* New York, NY: Viking, 2001.

Jonas, Gilbert. *Freedom's Sword: The NAACP and the Struggle Against Racism in America, 1909–1969.* New York, NY: Routledge, 2005.

Katz, William Loren, ed. *Thirty Years of Lynching in the United States, 1889–1918.* New York, NY: Arno Press, 1969.

Kaufman, Michael T. "Stokely Carmichael, Rights Leader Who Coined 'Black Power,' Dies at 57." *New York Times*, November 16, 1998. Retrieved December 7, 2013 (http://www.nytimes.com/1998/11/16/us/stokely-carmichael -rights-leader-who-coined-black-power-dies-at-57.html).

ABOUT THE AUTHOR

Diane Bailey has written about forty nonfiction books for children and teens on topics including sports, celebrities, government, finance, and technology. She has long been interested in both human rights and the American experience, and she was excited to discover the story of an organization that had such a profound influence during an important time in U.S. history. Bailey has written several manuscripts for novels for children, and she also works as an editor for other children's authors. She has two sons and two dogs, and she lives in Kansas. Her website is http://www.diane-bailey.com.

PHOTO CREDITS

Cover (Thurgood Marshall), p. 45 Hank Walker/Time & Life Pictures/Getty Images; cover (background), pp. 21, 32–33 Library of Congress Prints and Photographs Division; pp. 4–5 Nicholas Kamm/AFP/Getty Images; p. 9 Library of Congress Manuscript Division. Courtesy of the NAACP; pp. 12, 14, 51 MPI/Archive Photos/Getty Images; p. 16 Buyenlarge/Moviepix/Getty Images; pp. 18, 30 Hulton Archive/Archive Photos/Getty Images; p. 23 Jun Fujita/Hulton Archive/Getty Images; pp. 25, 37, 50, 55, 62 © AP Images; p. 27 Metronome/Archive Photos/Getty Images; p. 34 Universal Images Group/Getty Images; p. 41 Don Cravens/Time & Life Pictures/Getty Images; p. 44 Carl Iwasaki/Time Life Pictures/Getty Images; p. 47 AFP/Getty Images; p. 53 Bentley Archive/Popperfoto/Getty Images; p. 60 Chris Pizzello/Invision/AP Images; p. 64 John Angelillo/UPI/Landov; cover and interior background images © iStockphoto.com/Victor Pelaez (U. S. Constitution facsimile), © iStockphoto.com/klikk (American flag).

Designer: Nicole Russo; Editor: Andrea Sclarow Paskoff;
Photo Researcher: Amy Feinberg